"The Struggle Within…

My Sharpest *Thorn*"

Shronda Allen

H.I.S. Identity Coach

The Struggle Within… My Sharpest Thorn

Copyright © 2022 by Shronda Allen

ISBN (979-8-9858809-3-9)

Disclaimer: The following versions of the Bible may have been referenced: New International Version (NIV), King James Version (KJV), New Living Translation (NLT), English Standard Version (ESV), New King James (NKJV), New International Reader's Version (NIRV), Christian Standard Bible (CSB), Common English Bible (CEB), The Message (MSG).

MTE Publishing — mtepublishing.com

Dedication

This book is dedicated to EVERYONE who has struggled with their identity and are still finding their way.

Table of Contents

Chapters

Special Thanks & Acknowledgements

First, I thank God for everything that I have been through! I am who I am purposed to be because of God's plans navigated my life. Now, I am able to help others who share this struggle. Thank you, HOLY SPIRIT, for giving me the words to write and speak. Your guidance helped me through this process especially when I didn't understand. I *didn't have* the courage or boldness to write this book alone… But WITH You, the truth of who I am in you has now been told!

To my family, no part of my painful truth is intended to cast fault or blame. My story includes sexual abuse and candidly unpacks my sexuality. I am so thankful for the support and love you all have given me throughout my life.

Special thanks to my children Adrianna and Ashley, I love you unconditionally! I am so grateful for my grandparents, the Late Freddie Robinson and Mildred Robinson, Jasper and Salliemae (deceased) Allen, my mom Judy King and Jasper Allen Jr. my dad.

I genuinely appreciate my spiritual leaders, the Late Prophet Ken Gates, and Apostle Tanaka Gates of Victorious Life International, Inc.

I must recognize my friend, Denise! Thanks for always encouraging me to WRITE even when you did not understand my process! Lastly, thank you, Mrs. Kandra Albury for your continual encouragement. I am so grateful!

Foreword

I won't ask if life has been unbearable at times. However, I would like to know what we should do when it *seems* like God has turned a deaf ear to our prayers and covered His eyes during the tragedies in our life. We really do experience things that cause us to question God! However, I know God never sleeps on us in any capacity, and my mother, the author of this book is the proof!

My mother's life is her testimony and God's purpose for her life in progress. She has faced homosexuality, and she is now free in Christ. She struggled as a young single mom raising me and my sister as she worked two jobs and pursued higher education. The example she provided, taught me to be resilient, forgiving, and loving… Most importantly, she taught me how to stay connected to God, no matter what happens in my life!

I know this book will help every individual that takes the time to read it; because when we release our struggles to God, His strength is perfected, and our purpose is manifested. This literary work proves that God uses our thorns to help us fulfill our destiny.

Ashley Allen-Jones,

Daughter of Shronda Allen

Introduction

"Create in me a clean heart and Renew a right spirit within me."

~Psalms 51:10~

The scripture above is one of my favorite scriptures. I prayed this scripture *even* when my life was out of control. I knew what I desired God to do in my life and I cried out to Him. After I read Cindy Trimm's book, *40 Day Fast*, God dealt with me about being different. Initially, I wasn't receptive because I was worried about what people would say or think. Ironically, this is when I knew God created me to be different because I am predestined to reach certain people.

When I started writing, I asked God… "Besides telling my life story, what else do you want me to say?" The Holy Spirit dealt with me, and I was led to write about homosexuality (my sharpest thorn) because I still struggle, yet I love

God completely. Although, I am truly dedicated to God's will for my life, my thorn didn't dislodge after I committed my life to God. I have faced several obstacles along the way, However, facing myself is the factor that helped me with this literal confession.

I've always journaled my feelings because I didn't have anyone to talk with, so writing is my release. For years, my best friend told me, "Shronda you need to write the book!" I always agreed because I knew eventually I would. On November 28, 2016, Pastor Winter Brown told me to WRITE, WRITE, WRITE. I took her words as confirmation, and I started writing again. Then I contacted Mrs. Kandra Albury to guide me through the process.

I must admit this has not been an easy road. The enemy came like a lion, and it wasn't just roaring; I was attacked unmercifully, and I was ready to leave the church *again*. I constantly told myself I wasn't going back and prayed John 8:44, "The devil is a liar."

I hope everyone who reads this book is encouraged to keep pressing forward no matter what. People will not understand what God is doing in your life, but when God changes us, it is always evident. Our journeys will not to be like anyone else's, God wrote customized plans for each of us. Although, the enemy will attack us, God's plans are final. Don't give up, our journeys are purposeful and always worth it!

Love Always,

Shronda

"For our struggle is not against flesh and blood,
but against the rulers, against the authorities,
against the powers of this dark world and against
the spiritual forces of evil in the heavenly realms."

Ephesians 6:12 NIV

Chapter 1

It Started in Third Grade

I grew up in the small rural town of Micanopy, Florida. It is 11 miles south of Gainesville. It was a community with no strangers, and most folks were related. I loved to play sports and climb the oak trees! I only wore dresses when I went to church, I had no choice. I was quite the tomboy. My favorite sports were basketball, softball, and track.

During my early childhood years, I was raised by my grandparents and my Aunt Anita. I had a good childhood and my family ensured that I was loved. However, I do understand that no matter who *or* where we come from, we all have issues. I have emotional scars that indicate I've been hurt and at times the pain has tried to resurface. During these moments of emotional turmoil, I didn't know if I was coming or going, and I had these battles at a very young age.

Why Doesn't My Momma Want Me?

Growing up, I was emotionally detached from my mom. She had me at a young age. My mom grew up in a different era. Teenage pregnancy wasn't flaunted or applauded, it was shameful and hidden. However, I didn't understand the "whys" of several things. I felt unwanted by my mother, and I wanted answers. Quite frequently, I thought, "Why doesn't my momma want me? Does this have anything to do with *who* my dad is?" I needed answers, because I was innocent and I felt like I was being punished, and the sentence was more than harsh. I didn't want to be a motherless and unloved child. I understood that love was (and is) an action, but I didn't feel this from her. So, I frequently lashed out and acted out because I wanted my mom's attention.

In my late twenties, I finally realized my mom didn't know how to show affection towards me, but I still didn't understand what made me so different from my sisters? Finally, I just gave it to God and let Him handle it, but I still felt the same. I continued to grapple with these feelings as I got older. I just couldn't understand why me, and my mom's relationship had to be *that* way. However, I couldn't go to my grandmother because she was, *and still is* old school.

My Sharpest Thorn Pierced Me Early...

I was in second grade when I started to have *feelings* towards females, and I started to *look* at them, almost studying them. I despised seeing a woman being mistreated in person or on television. I looked at women in a way that I didn't understand, and I couldn't articulate *this* attraction at the time.

It was difficult for me to make sense of anything in my life… and when my half-brother started molesting me, I was beyond confused! I don't know why he introduced me to sex, his sister. I didn't even know what he was doing was called sex. My life was routine and all I knew was church, home, school, and repeat. I wasn't exposed to anything or anyone that could harm me, or so I thought.

As a nine-year-old girl, my brother introduced me to things I shouldn't have had any knowledge of. My brother forced himself inside me anally. I will never forget *that* day. We were at his aunt's house in his room. My brother and I did get along, so we played together. On this terribly unforgettable day, he told me to take off my clothes. By this time, he had been fondling me for a while. I did as I was told and took off my clothes. After I undressed, he told me to get in the bed. Then he put Crisco oil on his penis and Vaseline on me. He forced himself as I cried and clung to the bed. The pain was excruciating and when he finished, he told me to go home and wash with vinegar. He finished raping me right before his aunt walked into the house.

Before I left, he said, "You better not tell anybody, ever… and if you do, no one will believe you anyway!" He continued to violate me like this until I was in the 5th grade, and he wasn't the only one.

He stopped because I finally told! I was tired of him making me do things I didn't want to do. By this time, I had started my menstruation and sex-education, so I knew this had to stop. While attending Prairie View Elementary School, I told a teacher that I became fond of. I knew she genuinely cared about me and loved me. I felt comfortable and safe with her. I believed I could tell her about anything.

When I confessed the nature of my secret and how long I had kept it, she informed my fifth-grade teacher. Then they told my grandparents and my mom... Seemingly, my life spiraled downhill from this point.

A deputy came to my grandparents' house, and he questioned me while he stood in the kitchen. My brother's aunt was also there. I told the officer what happened. Strangely, I still felt helpless, and it was *still* my word against his. I was NOT taken to a hospital to be examined or anything! My world crushed me, and I felt like no one was on my side! Why was I treated as if I had brought this on myself? At this point, nothing *really* mattered to me anymore.

Since no one believed me regarding my brother, I never told anyone (until now) about a neighbor who violated me as well. He introduced me to oral sex, and I had my first orgasm at the age of ten. I never told anyone that my brothers' uncle molested me (but didn't penetrate me) from the ages 10-12. He gave me money every time he felt on me. This is how I thought love was supposed to go. In my mind, I was supposed to have sex, get paid, and *this* attention meant the person loved me.

I learned how to love in all the *wrong ways*. A portal was opened, and I didn't have the capacity to understand it. I became promiscuous, and I used people for what they could do for me, and I found myself attracted to older men. I was searching for validation and love. I got pregnant not once but twice.

My first pregnancy occurred when I was 14 years old. My family was disappointed and ashamed, and so was I. All the plans I made for myself were gone down the drain. I couldn't go into the military and that big house on 5 acres of land I dreamt I'd own by the time I was twenty-five, was also a lost cause.

At the age of seventeen, I became a ward of the courts, and I got an apartment. The former director of the ACCEPT program at Loften High School helped me. I continued my high school education, and I got my first job. My family also helped me a lot with my kids, and I successfully graduated and earned my high school diploma. My daughters are now twenty-four and twenty-three years old… and they are doing well for themselves.

Note: *If your child informs you that someone has touched them inappropriately, please listen to your child. Don't take it lightly! Let your child know they don't have to be afraid to talk to you.*

"A confused mind is a confused heart, and a confused heart is a confused mind."

~Shronda Allen

Chapter 2

Did God Make Me *This* Way?

I've asked myself repeatedly, "God, did you really make me this way?" My sexuality wasn't some habit a picked up in life, like when I used to smoke. Most people have heard the cliché, *God made Adam and Eve not Adam and Steve*, right? Well... this saying makes me cringe every time I hear it, I can't stand it! I know God created everyone in His image. Additionally, Genesis 1:31 reads, *Then God saw everything that He had made, and indeed it was very good.* I am God's creation and He made me for a reason.

I have thought about how God took Adam's rib and created Eve; therefore, women and men must possess some of the same characteristics, *right?* Now, Eve was not an infant when God created her from Adam's rib, she was a grown woman. This caused me to think about my DNA, lineage. and generational curses?

Homosexuality was practiced in biblical days, and the following scriptures highlight it: *"Do not have sexual relations with a man as one does with a woman". Leviticus 18:22 or in Romans 1:26b "Even their women exchanged natural sexual relations for unnatural ones" and Romans 1:27b "Men committed shameful acts with other men and received themselves the due penalty for their error."* Evidently God knew homosexuality would be someone's thorn, even before we were here! Otherwise, biblical scholars such as the Apostle Paul would not have written about it. And guess what? We are a part of their DNA, and we are heirs of Abraham.

I am not a scientist or a theologian/biblical scholar and I'm not making excuses. However, when I talk to God, I've always asked, "Lord if homosexuality is an abomination in your word, why do I have these feelings? Why was I attracted to women at such a young age? Why did you make this way? I wasn't exposed to lesbianism. What is really going on?"

I know there are several people (young and old) who have asked the same questions. I don't have the answers, but my life has allowed me to see everything that has transpired in my life is for God's GLORY! Homosexuality is my sharpest thorn, and I am not condemned because of it. God loves me just the same and is using me because of my testimony.

My initial attraction to girls occurred when I was in 3rd grade. However, I didn't act on my feelings until I was in high school. After having two children and being in love with my baby daddy, I was still attracted to women, and I did not understand why. So, I researched what was going on with me. I went to the library, and I found books that discussed different people who were "gay," but there was nothing that told me why I was attracted to women. Then I studied Sodom and Gomorrah intently. God destroyed these two cities because of sin not because of homosexuality.

Let me pause here because I've heard this lie since I was a kid. However, when I researched and studied for myself, I learned that God did not destroy the city just because of homosexuality. Sodom and Gomorrah were destroyed because of sin [Gen. 19:1-17, Jude 1:7] and pride [Ezekiel 16: 48-50]. I pray that people will read and meditate on the word for themselves and not just go on with the hype.

Even after years of hearing the debate of "people are not born gay" or "it's just a fad or a phase…" Please believe me, it is not that simple! I know I am going to get backlash from this, but I believe that people are born "gay." There is nothing in the bible that I've read that explicitly states people are not born being homosexuals. In *Psalm 139:13 NIV it states, "For you created my inner-*

most being: you knit me together in my mother's womb". Therefore, I know God knitted me together. God knows everything about me but more importantly, God created me to glorify Him with life by telling my story. So yes, I believe God made me this way to shut the mouths of the people that don't believe that God is still God, and He uses anyone that is willing… Guess what, telling my truth is my obedience to God and His will manifesting.

When I think of all the different disabilities and sickness that can develop while a child is in their mother's womb, I wonder why our sexual attractions are seemingly dismissed as genetic/hereditary traits. Everything about who we are is coded in our genes and our sexuality is not omitted from our genetic makeup.

As a child, I was overtaken with the desire to be a boy. I didn't know anything about gender reassignments or sex changes. I felt different because I was and am different. People condemn others too quickly without seeking to understand what a person is going through or why they feel the way they feel. I didn't understand my feelings or why women were so easily attracted to me rather than men? I was confused in my mind and heart. My heart wanted something that it was missing, and at the time, it was going after what it was seeking. So, my question is *still*, "Did God make me this way?" And although I pray and I fast, this thorn isn't budging. Now, I understand when we are honest with ourselves and God, things will change.

"Sometimes trying to prove there is a change will leave you in a worse state than you were in originally."
~Shronda Allen

Chapter 3

Straight. Gay. Straight, Repeat.

"I find then a law, that, when I would do good, evil is present with me. For I delight in the law of God after the inward man: But I see another law in my members, warring against the law of my mind, and bringing me into captivity to the law of sin which is in my members." Romans 7:21-25

I will never forget when I decided to give my life back to Christ in 2006. I had ended an unhealthy relationship and I was tired of being unhappy. I started attending church on Sundays and Wednesday nights for bible study. I was excited about being back in church and I felt a weight lift off of me. I told my kids I had gotten saved, and they were excited! I told them I was done with my lesbian lifestyle [they had never seen me with a man]. I meant this from my heart, and I was determined to live *right*.

In the meantime, I reconnected with someone from my past that I had not seen or heard from in years. His brother came through McDonald's drive-thru one night while I was working, and we begin to talk, and he mentioned his brother. I asked how he was doing, and he told me he was doing well. I gave my number to him for his brother to call me sometime.

As fate would have it, I did something that I said I would never do… I became involved with someone that was in prison. Well, I knew him from my past and at that time I wasn't trying to get into a relationship with any dude, but I did. We talked on the phone, and he wrote me letters. I barely wrote back because I wasn't into that, and I really didn't have time. He knew about my sexuality, but he said he didn't care because he always loved me. I was his "sugar bear" and he wanted to make me happy again. He apologized for not being there for me when we were younger… but we were kids, there wasn't much he could have done. We were both stuck in what could have been instead of what it was [presently].

I went to visit him in federal prison only once because I wasn't with that going back and forth. As he approached his release date, he was trying to decide if he would go home to Miami to live with his mom or stay close so we could be together. He went with the latter. While he was in the process of being released, I was in the process of changing. One of my mom's friend daughters had gotten married and my mom often said, "I will be glad when one on my children gets married." I would just laugh.

I changed quickly without any specific direction; I was going with the flow. I started getting my hair and nails done although I had never been into that at all. Then my wardrobe changed, and I wore capris and more feminine shirts. Honestly, I didn't have a problem with this because I had lost weight and I welcomed the attention. However, when I went around my family, I still felt uncomfortable… I felt like I had to prove I was no longer "gay" (I really don 't like using that word, I never labeled myself). So, in the process of making all these changes to prove I was *delivered* - I still battled on the inside.

The thorn was still lodged in my flesh… it was deeply embedded and sharp. I couldn't ignore it. I prayed and asked God to put scales over my eyes so that I would not see women as I usually see them. I also asked God, "If my feelings are wrong why do I and so many other people have them?

So, as I continued my cosmetic changes, my "boyfriend" was getting ready to come home and I needed to make sure I was *delivered.* I wanted to prove people wrong and show them what God had done in my life. Well, my boyfriend was on probation when he was released and had to live in Ocala. We still spent a considerable amount of time with each other. I went to Ocala to see him, and he came to church with me. We were happy and planned to get married. Everything was going well in my spiritual walk. I was spending time in prayer and reading my word. I really was trying to live this thing out…

After almost a year of my boyfriend being home, something unexpected happened. One evening I was on the phone with my best friend, who lives in Tennessee. I always made time to talk with her although our schedules always conflicted, and I didn't know when I'd have a chance to talk to her again.

My ex-fiancé called while we were talking, but I didn't answer the phone. I ignored the first couple calls, but he kept calling. So, I clicked over and told him I would call him back, but it didn't go well. When I ended my conversation with my best friend, I called him, and he went off! I tried to explain what was going on, but he refused to listen.

His words were venomous… and he called me every derogatory name he could think of. He spoke his heart; this was how he really felt. In so many words, he told me to go back to being with women among other things (I won't repeat his exact words).

The rage that festered within me was not good. I hung up on him, but he continued to call. When I didn't answer he left extremely vulgar and hurtful voicemails. The next morning when I got up it was on and poppin'. I was ready for war. I was going to kill him; he would be the last dude to hurt me! As I cried through the night, I told God, "I've done what YOU and everyone else wanted me to do… Now I am going to do things my way!"

At the time, I didn't own a gun, but I stormed into my kitchen and grabbed a knife while crying and talking to myself. I bashed myself for trying to do what was right. I didn't care about what *could* happen… I was on my way to Ocala.

My daughter saw me, and she hadn't ever

seen me *this* angry. So, she called one of my friends

and told her what was going on. When my friend

called me, I didn't answer. However, she called me

until I answered (I was driving through Micanopy

at the time). She talked and I actually listened.

When she told me that I needed to think about my

kids before I did something I'd regret, my

common sense returned, and my anger subsided.

As bad as I wanted to put my hands on him,

I turned around and drove back to Gainesville. I

went to my friend's house, and I cried profusely.

From that day forward, I looked at things

differently. Although I forgave him, I remained

angry for a long time. I never expected him to do

or say the things he did.

Eventually, I tried dating another guy and

he tried to fill my mind and heart with dreams, but

I wasn't having it. One night I saw him in Walmart

with his child and his other half. I was shocked

because he didn't even live in Gainesville because he was in the military. I didn't know anything about this visit or the other woman he was with… I was like whoa, "Okay, this is it. I'm done!" Although I was still attending church, my mind and soul were somewhere else. Instead of praying and asking God for help, I took matters into my own hands.

I wasn't looking to be with another female (that's what I kept saying to myself) but there was one that I just had to have. I wanted to prove that she was in the "life" because I had peeped it and I believed I could bring *it* out of her. Again, I wasn't looking for a relationship; I just wanted to be the one who helped her be honest with herself. Yes, I realized that I was wrong for this, and my actions were selfish. It was a thrill for me to prove that I could bring *it* out of her. I used my charming tactics to be with someone that I really didn't want because of the hurt and pain I felt. I had done this more than I care to admit, it was an unhealthy coping mechanism.

Then I realized I was doing more harm than good, and sooner or later I'd be held accountable for the things that I'd done. My actions proved I didn't love myself and that I had a problem with ME. The more I pondered the more I realized *this thorn* wasn't budging! I believed if I talked to someone, I'd be judged. My mind and heart were confused.

Note: *I've learned that I don't want to be like others because I want to be able to help people genuinely. My life isn't just talk, I have endured these battles and I have the testimony to prove it. Ultimately, I understand that change is up to the person, but I don't want to blindly push anyone out there. I want to help them navigate their path as God guides me. I had to fend for myself, and I know what's it's like.*

"Don't let the hypocrisy of people

define who you are."

~Shronda Allen

Chapter 4

The Hypocrisy of Homosexuality

When did homosexuality become the greatest sin? Is it the same as adultery or fornication? Is it in a category by itself? Let's examine this highly debated topic.

When I decided to come out, I didn't make a big announcement and say, "Hey everyone, I'm a lesbian." I went through a process for *this* change. I continued to go to church, and I was *still* attracted to women. I *still* felt the presence of God, and I knew God had not forsaken or left me (read that again).

One day I made up in my mind that I was going to break free and live my life [on my terms]. I was never feminine, so changing my wardrobe wasn't hard because I only wore dresses to church. I cut my long pretty hair that God (and DNA) blessed me with. Then I stopped going to church. Ironically, I experienced more turmoil when I came out than when I got pregnant. When "church folks" saw me outside of church they pretended like they didn't know me. My initial response was, "Wowwww!"

I stopped going to church because I refused to be mistreated. I remember going to church one Sunday because my daughter was doing a praise dance with the dance ministry; I loved seeing my girls perform. As I walked in church the greeters were passing out programs but guess who didn't get one? My appearance had changed, and I was no longer the young girl they knew. The hurt I felt was overwhelming and I just wanted to be accepted as a person – as Shronda.

I vowed to never step foot into church again, *unless* my grandmother invited me (even then I was still hesitant, but I can't tell my grandmother, no). I prayed and asked God to forgive those who mistreated me. I understand that no matter what, God commands us to love.

It's funny how people are, especially Christians, we can be so hypocritical. We tend to pick and choose what and who we will love and accept. Especially, when the "thing or person in question" knocks at our front door. I remember being around my mom and observing her behavior around my sister's open gay boss. She laughed and conversed with him without hesitation. However, when I think about how she is with my daughter and how she was with me, it was like night and day. I'm not saying that my mom didn't love us; I am saying our personal experiences with her as her lesbian daughter and granddaughter were noticeably different.

When my mom found out that my daughter was living an alternative lifestyle (which is what I prefer to call it) she felt like my daughter was going down the same path I did. Instead of talking to her grandchild and showing love towards her, she subtly attacked her and uttered the cliché, *"God made Adam and Eve, not Adam and Steve,"* among other things that really scarred my daughter. Their relationship has not been the same since.

Why do we pick and choose what we want to call sin? Why do so many people classify homosexuality as a *greater* sin than others? Listen! Sin is sin, no matter how we choose to classify it. Whether we commit adultery, fornication, stealing, lying, or whatever else that is against the word of God and His commandments, it is a sin.

I suppose the fornicating deacon who's slept with the married church secretary isn't so bad because the sin occurred in a heterosexual manner. And... the pastor or first lady who's having an affair with the musician is excusable because their sin occurred in a heterosexual manner too. For some reason or another, homosexuality is the most talked about and most ridiculed "sin" in the church. Ironically, within the Black church, several of the musicians and worship team members are gay. However, the church relies on them to usher in the presence of God… Go figure (Before Lucifer was thrown out of heaven, he was the chief musician)! STOP BEING A HYPOCRITE. PLEASE!

Here's what is wrong with the church today… We are too busy trying to please people instead of pleasing God. Consequently, we miss what is truly important. Souls being delivered and people experiencing the life-changing love of God! So, what kind of message are we sending? That it is okay to pretend to accept and love people as long as it's benefits us or the church in some way. No this is not right. If we are going to preach the word and live by the word, let's do that! Contrary to popular beliefs and practices, none of us have a heaven or hell to put anyone in!

When did homosexuality become the greatest sin? Do we really put sins in categories as if they are misdemeanors or felonies? Sometimes that's what it feels like, homosexuality is a first-degree felony and those charged with it must be ostracized and treated like black sheep. Where is the love in this…? I'll wait. We are supposed to love. JESUS never told or treated anyone as if they were unlovable, no matter what they did!

If we read the word of God and study it, we will realize that many religious practices and beliefs are manmade and filled with false ideals. Far too often, we turn our backs on homosexuals, drug addicts, homeless people, etc. This is not love. People should experience the love of God in everything we do. God doesn't exclude people from experiencing unconditional love. The people that claim to love God ostracize people. There are too many individuals hurting that want/need to be loved and we should be able to show compassion and love genuinely. Hey, it's what God commanded us to do. Please hear my heart. We all need to stop being hypocrites and follow God's word and example. If we work God's word, the word will work for and through us.

"We delight in the beauty of the butterfly, but rarely admit the changes it has gone through to achieve that beauty."

~ Maya Angelou

Chapter 5

Inside My Cocoon I *Still* Felt the Thorns

"The struggle to leave the cocoon is what strengthen the butterfly's wings, so she can fly." Tricia Stirling

When I think about the butterfly, I know that the transformation process starts inside of the cocoon. However, I had some malfunctions (thorns) before my transformation process started. I was hurting inside and felt neglected. Honestly, I believed I was the black sheep of my family. I felt like my existence was a mistake. I mean, I felt rejected by my family, so it was hard to believe that I would ever be accepted and loved.

At times, the pain was so unbearable that I contemplated suicide. I felt unwanted anyway! The molestation I endured did something to me, on the inside. I held so much anger and hurt. I was vulnerable and emotionally unstable. I was "easy"

and anyone who showed me attention had me –
almost instantly. I fell for these people because I
felt like they were the missing puzzle piece in my
life (love and acceptance).

These relationships took *something* from me,
but I settled because they provided the attention I
wanted. I fell for the wrong people, and I sought
love in all the wrong places. Naturally, I thought…
*If God loved me so much, why was I violated, unprotected,
and rejected (more thorns).* My innocence was stripped
away, and I was full of anger. My cocoon didn't
stop the thorns from puncturing me!

I was angry with the church and *so-called*
Christians. How could they claim to love God, yet
turn their backs on me? I was angry with my family
because I believed I should have been loved
unconditionally, no matter what the circumstances
of my life were. Later, I realized they didn't know
how to handle *their thorns or mine*… at that time.
Maybe no one did, life was different back then.

I felt these thorns physically, emotionally, and spiritually. However, within my cocoon was me, a person who knew how to love because I knew how I needed to be loved in return. I was taken advantage of because I have a good heart and I choose to see the good in people. I easily forgave those who hurt me, and I remained connected to these relationships because I hated being alone, and I desperately wanted acceptance. So, even when I knew people were using me, I didn't care because I considered them my friend.

I gave my heart away and I was hurt in the process. People knew I was reliable, even family! When they called, I was there no matter what the circumstances were. I was the ride or die type, but I didn't get that in return. I lost myself searching for love outside of God and myself. Although, I knew how to love, I loved for all the wrong reasons. I wasn't an attention seeker, or so I thought.

People were drawn to me, but I didn't understand why. I didn't do anything special… I was just me - the only way I knew to be authentically, truthfully, and godly. As I tell my painful truth, I am thankful for all of it because it allows me to help others accept and love themselves while understanding the need of the thorns.

I want people to experience (not just see) the true transformation God has done within me. God has done and is doing a marvelous work within me (daily). No one gets credit except God. I want the world to know that as we grow inside our cocoons, God is with us! We will feel the thorns but if we allow God to be God – we will see how every unfortunate circumstance in our lives eventually leads to the manifestation of God's plan and our destiny. The struggle(s) will seem unbearable, but no matter how difficult the process is, we must endure to reach our transformation. God has already established our expected end. Believe this: Sometimes our thorns are the very things that helps us break free from our cocoon!

*"Some choices you make will come with a battle,
because not everyone will agree with your decision."*

Chapter 6

My Choice, My Battle

The choices we make either start a battle or end a battle, so no matter what, we are always fighting. When I chose to break up with my daughter's father, I was tired of hiding how I really felt. I was tired of pretending with him because I wanted to be with a woman. Inevitably, I knew leaving him would be a battle. When I came out, I didn't say, "Hey, I'm gay." I went through stages. I was already tomboyish and if I remember correctly the only feminine trait, I had was my long hair. I even walked like a guy.

So, one of the first things I did was change my wardrobe. I knew exactly how I wanted to dress. When I looked at my reflection, I didn't think I was attractive. I wore big bifocals and I had terrible acne. However, I knew how I wanted to be treated, so I knew how I would treat *my* woman. I didn't care how anyone felt about my choice, I just wanted to be happy.

In 1996, I had my first real relationship. Finally, I was happily living my life as I wanted... but then I experienced a different battle(s). The young lady I was with for 5 years used to hit me because she knew I wasn't abusive (I refused to hit her). We went through a lot together and I endured so much with her. But… I loved her so none of the violence mattered until she hit me, *the last time.*

I knew that I had to put a stop to it before I lost my life. I let her first hit go, and I told her to stop. I never believed that a man should hit a woman or vice versa and I refused to take this type of abuse from her any longer! When we allow people to mistreat us, they believe it's ok to do just that.

Before same-sex marriages were legalized, I had already planned to marry her, but that all changed in an instant. I didn't know she was planning to leave me for another woman, and I was not prepared for this blow. How can we prepare for heartbreak? With this battle I chose to change for the worst… I was all about me! I didn't care who I hurt or who I *turned out*… I went in full throttle, whether they were straight, gay, bisexual, bi-curious. Simply put, I didn't care.

I had been hurt… so it was time to pass the buck. While in Job Corps, I developed a reputation that preceded me and although I wasn't proud of it, I figured at least people knew what they were getting. I was turning girls out left and right. They wanted to know what it was like to be with a woman, so I gave it to them. I didn't care about their dudes, and I wished someone would approach me about it. I was so out of control that one day the director Job Corps told me I had to go. I had gotten my two trades and my money, so I left.

Although I put up a hardened front, I was really ashamed of my choices. As the years went by, I made other choices that proved my brokenness. I drank, smoked, and used cocaine... something I never thought I would do. I was a functioning addict. I battled with myself and others constantly because I didn't realize or recognize who I was in Christ.

Reality slapped me in the face the day I almost lost my job. I decided I would get high one more time for my birthday. This was the birthday I would go out with a bang! Well, that's exactly what happened when I was called in for a random drug test. I knew I was about to lose everything, and it was no one's fault but mine. But God was on my side, and He had mercy on me. Instead of losing my job, I was given another chance as long as I attended NA meetings and remained clean.

I was so ashamed, and I didn't want to go. I was afraid someone would see me. My reasoning was quite selfish. I wasn't thinking about my children at all. However, I quickly snapped out of that mindset because my children needed me! I didn't tell anyone what was going on with me. I understood my choices would only bring me up or down, so I chose an upward progression.

Instead of your shame you shall have double; and instead of confusion they shall rejoice in your position: therefore, in their land they shall possess double: everlasting joy shall be unto them. Isaiah 61:7 (KJV)

Chapter 7

My Shame & My Honor

July 7, 2008, Diary entry:

If I refuse to acknowledge that I have fallen and I am separated from God, who is my eternal source, I will find myself in a fallen condition unable to get up. Though now I am like Nebuchadnezzar I refuse to ask for God's help because I am ashamed, and I don't want to continue to fall. (Daniel 4:34-36,37)

To fall is bad enough but to fall and not cry out for help, refusing to repent for my sin is worst than the fall itself. I don't think it's my pride or maybe it is. I'd rather not ask for help to avoid people's judgement. Guess what? I have proven them right. Yes, I temporarily convinced myself that no one would know. But I know and God knows the sins I have committed. I don't want to remain in a state of self-deception. Nor do I want my pride to bury me in a state of unforgiveness.

I have fallen and gotten back up again… But I don't want to continue this see-saw cycle of going up and down. I want to live for God – authentically. So, Lord please hear me. I need you to remove this thorn from my flesh. This hindering spirit that's keeping me from living for you. Lord, I give you honor and glory for my change and I thank you for doing it now. Amen.

This is what I prayed because I really wanted to change. I wanted people to see and know what God had done and what He was *still* doing in my life. I wanted the people to know that they could change too…no matter what that change was! We all have done things that we're ashamed of. Things that make us thank God for mouthless walls.

However, I am so grateful that the shame I have experienced has granted me double honor! I have a second chance at life. I have another chance to get it right while possibly helping someone else. I am honored to know that this book is proof that

God is for me and with me. I am truly about my Father's business. There are individuals who have stated I wouldn't make but I am here! My relationship with God is REAL.

When I stopped trying to prove what God had done and is doing for me… I became liberated in simply being who God created me to be. God didn't need my help… my obedience and willingness to trust God moved Him on my behalf. My deliverance is *not* in the removal of my thorn – it is me accepting who I am and being wise enough to know that my need of God keeps me humble. Therefore, the thorns in my life – even the sharpest ones are necessary! I get joy every time I tell my testimony because it's not about me, this is about God's love for me!

I have received backlash because I don't "look" delivered. What does deliverance look like anyway? Sinners don't have a specific wardrobe or look… and last I checked none of us are without thorns – whether we are saints or sinners. I would rather wear jeans, a polo shirt, and tennis shoes being who I am - with issues. I am not holier than Thou and I will not pretend to be. But beyond my clothes (my exterior) the glory of God dwells within me and it radiates externally! When I speak to others they listen, and they commend me for being honest. However, I let them know it's not about me it's all about God and what He is doing in my life.

I count it an honor to be a representative of God's love. I felt ashamed for so long that I didn't understand my worth. I didn't realize God had already set me up for *my greater*. Everything that I've endured has prepared me for what God has in store… I know I have a double portion coming. I am not in this walk alone. No matter what I face or struggle with – God accepts me, God loves me, and I was placed here for God's use. When we accept that our lives are in God's hands, God gives us the strength to conquer the very things we thought would overtake us. No more shame… I've chosen to embrace the honor that God has given me.

Chapter 8

What God Promises... God Fulfills

I know I am delivered because I know where God has brought me from; nevertheless, my journey continues. I will be honest, my journey to become who God created me to has not been easy. I have fallen several times and I've gotten up every time! When I share my testimony, I experience the most turmoil, but I am prepared and ready! Now, I remain focused, and I don't give into my desires – (we are led astray by our own desires – nothing else, James 1:14 NIV).

I separated myself from people I knew would bring me down. I had to go through the pain of enduring the thorns of loneliness and selfishness. This process didn't feel good because I didn't want to be alone. I wanted to bring my friends (the little I had) with me. I wanted them to feel what I felt. More importantly, I wanted them to know that no matter what God loves and accepts them too!

Unfortunately, it didn't always work so ideally. Some of them said things like, "Oh you're holier than thou now" or "It don't take all of that." Their words were hurtful, but I knew I couldn't do the work for them. I simply hoped they saw what God had done within me and believed He'd do the same for them.

We all have issues. My journey will not be like anyone else's and I'm finally okay with this. My process has been long and tedious. Often, I felt like giving up, but God didn't let me go. I would get upset with myself because I felt I wasn't progressing fast enough. I didn't want my deliverance on man's terms… My exodus had to happen on God's terms. I have been tried and tested and I have failed miserably, but I am not defeated. I don't want to straddle the fence. I want the ministry God has placed within me to be like no other. I want people to know that God loves them for real! So, the presentation of my message has to look and sound different! People like me need to know that God loves people like us – JUST THE SAME!

Understanding our struggles and recognizing the need of the thorns helps us recognize our need of God so remain humble. God has planned every aspect of our lives, the good, the bad, and everything in between. Although, we will want to give up some days, God will remind us of how far we've come. So, forgive yourself because our Father has already forgiven you. Maintain your relationship with God and ask Him to guide you. Please understand, our thorns are not an indication that God has left us… but they prove God is with us!

A Letter to Parents

Dear Parents:

If you have a child that is living an alternative lifestyle, I want to encourage you, that you are not alone, and you have support. I know it's hard to accept things we don't expect or simply don't want to accept. Internally, you may have thought, *"I didn't raise him/her like this and where did this come from?"*

I know it may hurt, but your son/daughter needs to know that you love them, no matter what! Now more than ever, they need to know that if no one else loves them, at least their family does! The ridicule and rejection from outsiders are difficult to endure but feeling rejected within your family is unbearable.

I have a daughter that is in the "life" and when I first found out, I cried. Then, I asked God 'how could this happen?' I didn't want *this* for her.

Although I knew in my spirit this was going to happen, I didn't want it to. I saw it before she did, and it wasn't that she was *tomboy-ish* or anything like that, I just knew. Even in my sin, I prayed about this, and I was heartbroken. I felt as though God didn't answer my prayer because I was in my own sin.

When I got myself together, I talked with my daughter and asked her what made her go *this* route. I knew she had a boyfriend and boys were attracted to her and vice versa. I thought maybe I had done something wrong, and I questioned my parenting. Where did I mess up? However, my daughter explained to me (in her eyes) I had done everything right! She told me that had developed feelings for a young lady at school. After we talked, I thanked her for opening up and I told her that I loved her no matter what and I'd always be there for her. I vowed to protect her from the things I went through, and I meant that! I pray for her, I encourage her, and I will never turn my back on her.

Parents I encourage you to be there for your son or daughter. Regardless of what it looks like… stick by them. When a child doesn't have the support from their parents, they become rebellious because they're hurt! Please don't be the cause of your child distancing themselves from you and God. We are loved by God even when we don't deserve it! He is there for us. So, I encourage you to pray for and with your son or daughter and God will bring them out. Keep the faith and continue interceding on their behalf. Thank you for hearing my heart and I pray this book has blessed you.

About the Author

Shronda Allen is a Florida native who has tenaciously strived for greater! She is a mother, entrepreneur, nurse, a sincere servant to people and now a published author.

Shronda wrote, "The Struggle Within… My Sharpest *Thorn*" to encourage others that there is nothing more liberating than placing our lives in the divine sovereignty of God. When we do this our lives are destined to move in an upward trajectory. With God we can't lose.

In her spare time, Shronda enjoys serene outings at the beach, intentional time with God, and spending with family and friends.